God's Hand Upon My Life:
New Edition

Georgia M. Carroll

GOD'S HAND UPON MY LIFE

By Georgia M. Carroll

Printed in the United States of America

ISBN: 979-8-89860-497-4

Imprint: Independently published

Illustrations are all AI generated from Microsoft Copilot.

Dedication and Tribute

I want to dedicate this book to: Rev. Ronald L. Bobo, Sr., D. Min. He serves as Senior Pastor of the Westside Missionary Baptist Church. A man of visionary leadership, he has challenged our congregation to (Take This City for God). His desire is to (share hope) in a hopeless world.

Through listening to numerous C.D.s by our pastor, I was inspired to write my life story. One of his C.Ds in particular entitled (Born in the Wilderness) was taken from scripture- Joshua 5:1-12. He stated in that sermon, not because you were so great, but because God was doing great things in you, for you, and through you. He encouraged his listeners to tell their story of what God has done for them.

"If God brought you out, you need to tell your story in such a way people will know it wasn't because of your efforts. But it was because of God's hand upon your life."

Therefore, this book is entitled, "God's Hand Upon My Life." Also, this book is dedicated to a mother and daughter team in the gospel, Mrs. Bessie Spigner and her daughter, Angel Roberts; Ministers of God that worked with me at Northview Nursing

Home. We held services for the residents. They were so encouraging and inspiring to my ministry with serving residents.

Also, my children, Macie M. Strong (oldest daughter,) Sherri R. Girma (second daughter,) Vanessa B. Strong (third daughter,) and DeAndre L. Strong (only son,) my son-in-law Bekele Girma and my grandchildren- Lea Rahael Girma (oldest granddaughter,) Christian Azana Bekele Girma (oldest grandson); Takisha Andrea Strong (second granddaughter,) Nadia (granddaughter in law,) Zairea Strong (granddaughter,) Andre' Allen Strong (second grandson,) and Sherika (granddaughter in law). And thanks to my cousin Mrs. Linda M. Buggs-Simms who was so inspirational in putting this book together and typing the manuscript.

Most of all, I thank God for letting me live to write my story.

About this Book

(God's Hand Upon My Life) shares how God's hand has been upon my life from childbirth through my teens and as an adult mother and Christian. I also, share my journey of being hospitalized to other aspects of my life. In my early twenties, I thought God was getting ready to call me home. But he spared me to raise my children and see them grow up to adulthood.

To everyone that read this book, it is my prayer that you accept Christ as your Lord and Savior according to Romans 10:9-11.

Romans 9:10-11: That if you confess with your mouth the Lord Jesus and believe in your heart that God has raised him from the dead, you will be saved.

Romans 10: For with the heart one believes unto righteousness and with the mouth, confession is made unto salvation.

Romans 11: For the scripture says, "whoever believes on him will not be put to shame."

Birth Place: Pace, Mississippi
Date: January 2, 1937
Father: Rev. George Carroll
Mother: Estella Mae Green

My birth was quite controversial as it caused a lot of confusion due to my father was the pastor of the church and my mother was seventeen years old. The church called a meeting and was going to impeach my father, but he brought one of his brothers to the meeting. His name was Thomas Carroll. I met him some years later and he told me that he told them at the meeting that he was my father and not his brother George Carroll. My Aunt Carrie told me a lady, which was one of the members, came to her home with a butcher knife looking for me. Aunt Carrie said they hid me, so she left. But God's hand was upon my life, even as an infant.

However, God spared my life. I was told by two cousins that when I was a small infant I would cry so much, until when my mother went to the field to work, they would pour red pepper in my mouth so much that they had to wash it down with water to keep my mother from noticing it. Yes, God's hand has always been upon my life.

Years later in a conversation with my mother, she realized keeping me was not possible so she packed my things and sent me to live with my grandmother, Alberta Brown-Nevette at the age of 9 months.

My grandmother had a young daughter seven years my senior, which was autistic due to experiencing spasms at an early age.

So, I grew up with Jennie V, which sometimes handled me in very dangerous ways.

We lived in Mississippi, until I was about four years old. During my stay in Mississippi, I remember quite a few things that I experienced going with Jennie V. We went to pump water from the plantation owner and one day someone from the house fired shots at us. Then we ducked behind a big tree. One day, Jennie and me was coming back to the house and a German Shepherd dog started chasing us. I ran down in a ditch, but he caught Jennie and bit her. When he went away, I came up out of the ditch and followed Jennie home.

Jennie's father, Bud Nevette, lived with us. He was so angry that he went after the dog to kill him. I don't remember if he did. There were other times I remember in Mississippi, like when we picked cotton. I was given 3 quarters, so I bought ice cream bars for myself, my two aunts, and for my grandmother.

Then there were times when we would end up in a truck with chairs going to hear Bishop Mason preach. I remember him well because he came to Missouri and preached on the riverbanks at baptismal services.

Eventually my grandmother's oldest daughter, Mary Watson and her family moved to St. Louis, MO. Aunt Mary, would write letters to my grandmother telling her to move up to St. Louis, MO.

She said we could stay with her and her family until we found a place to live.

So, we finally packed what few things we could and caught a train to St. Louis, MO. Aunt Mary was waiting for us and we went to her home. I remember the number 808 North Jefferson.

I was so happy to be there because my three cousins: Rosie Mae, Sammy and George (called Junior,) was also there. They treated me like their little sister. I felt protected when I was with them.

Soon I was five and they had to enroll me in school. I was enrolled in Banneker Elementary School, where Mr. Hunter became the principal. That is where I had been going to with my cousins and Jennie V. One day at recess, I thought school was out. So, I followed the way I had walked with my cousins until I got to my house.

Aunt Mary was shocked to see me and asked me where my cousins were. I told her I did not know. So, she kept me with her until her children came home. She hid me and asked her children where I was. They started explaining to her that they did not see me and that they had looked everywhere. They were almost in tears. She finally called me out from hiding and they were so shocked to see me. I think I would have gotten a few punches had Aunt Mary not been in the room.

While living with Aunt Mary, we attended Bostick Temple Church of God in Christ.

When I was 7 years old, I went to the altar and accepted Christ. Soon, we had the annual baptismal service, as accustomed down at the Mississippi River. There was a lot of people to be baptized! I was the first in line because I was the youngest. Bishop Mason was preaching on the riverbanks, while Bishop Bostick held me up and then pronounced, in the name of the Father, in the name of the son and Holy Ghost, in Jesus' name, and I went under. Even though I was young, I remember being baptized in the Father, Son, and Holy Ghost.

I was really amazed at Bishop Mason; he was highly anointed with the Holy Spirit. So much, until the point where the church that he pastored in in the south had crutches and wheel chairs where people had been healed and left them in the church!

We stayed with Aunt Mary's a while until my grandmother was able to find a job. Sometime after that my grandmother, her daughter and me moved out because Aunt Mary was always making room in her home for other relatives from the south. She was very instrumental providing space in her home as others migrated from the south.

After we moved, Jennie V's father came to St. Louis and stayed with us. One night he passed away and my grandmother and Jennie V went over to Aunt Mary's house to get her while they were gone. I thought my grandfather gave me an apple. When they returned Aunt Mary took the apple and disposed of it. They had to cremate him because he did not have insurance and the family was unable to pay for a funeral and burial.

We moved quite a few times and finally changed churches. We joined Holy Ghost Tabernacle where Elder Gullett was the pastor. I felt so loved at that church by sister Gullett. They had three daughters. The oldest, Camille Gullett. They had three daughters. The oldest, Patricia, second Natola and the third C.B. I never knew CB's real name. Sister Gullett treated me just as if I was her own child.

One day we were having a shut-in prayer and fasting service. Some of my sisters were there. My mother had given one lady advice not to let me sit with my sisters. So, when Sister Gullett found out what she had done she really got down on her and told her she needed to get saved if she felt the way she did about her own child.

While attending Holy Ghost Tabernacle some of the children was given gleaners. These were little card board papers that held dimes. With those we went out in our neighborhood asking for money for the church. One night my grandmother had a dream. In the dream she said it was wrong for the children to go out asking for money.

Elder Gullett was upset with her after she told the dream in church. So, he silenced her and would not let her participate in the services, dancing, and testifying. One Sunday my grandmother was anointed and started to dance. She danced up toward the pulpit where Elder Gullett was and began to wave her hands toward him rebuking him. I never told my grandmother because I was afraid. But she was right about not sending children out to ask for money because one day when Jennie V and me went to glean money. Jennie V got in front of me and was about a block from me and I asked a man to help me on the church offering. He took my hand and started leading me into an alley. I don't know what his intentions were, but when he started down some stairs, I was able to break free and I ran. God's hand was upon my life, and I was able to get away from him.

Right after that episode in church, my grandmother decided to change churches, so we started going to

507 South Jefferson Church where Rev. James Ward was the pastor. After that demonstration of the Holy Ghost, Elder Gullett began experiencing tremendous problems.

While attending (507), I met the O'Neal twins. They were singers. One of them, Edgar O'Neal, played the piano and his brother, Edward O'Neal, lead most of the songs. After being at the church for a few years, I went to talk to the pastor about starting a choir. Pastor Ward said it would be all right if we did not start trouble, because of the choir. So, we started a choir and became known as the Ward Specials. We had quite a few singers, some very good. One of the singers was Charles, another Dora Lee, another Ann, and her sister Nel, Wilderdeen, and her sisters. Even though we had not been singing long, God blessed our group until we were in demand by other churches (Bostick Temple, Kennerly Temple, and others.)

The O'Neal Twins mother, Rowena, asked me if I would like to sing with her sons Edward and Edgar. I agreed and she started picking me up and taking me to sing with them. She always gave me money. I also was attending Benneker School where I met Lawrence Craig a very nice boy that played the piano and sang.

Lawrence gave me his address and told me that his mother was a music teacher, because I was interested in learning to play the piano.

I told my grandmother that I wanted to take piano lessons from Mrs. Craig. She agreed and I started taking lessons. Mrs. Craig also had a group called the Craig Specials, consisting of her son, Lawrence, Bertha White, Fontella Bass, Zerline and her sister Edna and me.

Mrs. Craig was our sponsor so she took us to make appearances on different programs. I did not learn to play the piano very well, but I enjoyed singing in her group.

Later in my teens, I started a singing trio consisting of me, Delores Williams and Mary Rodgers. We were called the Gospelettes. We were doing quite well because Mary could also play the piano. Whenever we sang at my church. The pastor's son (James Ward, Jr.) would run up to sing with us. I let him sing but Mary and Delores were somewhat disgusted because we had rehearsal on the songs we sang. But that was my little sonny. (smile)

In the year 1951 January, I graduated from Banneker Elementary School. After graduation, my Aunt Mary decided she wanted to go to Detroit, Michigan to visit her sister Carrie. She wanted to take me with her. I was permitted to go with her.

Aunt Carrie was waiting for us when we arrived. We spent a few days with her and then my Aunt Mary decided that she wanted to go to my father's church so we went to a service at his church. They treated us real nice and when they found out that I was a singer they called me up to sing. My father had not arrived at that time but my Aunt Carrie told me that she would hunch me when he came.

But a few minutes after I sang, I looked back at the door and a tall dark man came in and I recognized him immediately that he was my father. So, when Aunt Carrie hunched me and told me "that is your old man" coming in, I said yes I know. I guess I knew him because we looked so much alike.

We ended up going to my father's house to spend a night. I was leery of his wife, and his daughter Mary had a little boy named Lawrence. He seemed to like me quite a lot. He kept coming to me and his grandmother said Lawrence likes little black girls. Her maid said "his grandmother like black men." I was told not to tell my name was Georgie Mae Carroll. But I called myself Joycie Jean Gray.

When we left their house, my father came over to Aunt Carrie's house to see me again. He was really nice to me and when he left, he said he would see me again.

Aunt Mary received a call from her daughter Rosie, asking her to come home because she was having domestic problems, so we packed up and returned to St. Louis.

Before going to Detroit, we had been spelling my name "Cail" but my father told me it should be spelled "Carroll." So, I had to get my name spelled right when I attended Vashon High School.

Enrolling in Vashon, I joined the band. I really enjoyed the band; I got the chance to wear pants. I remained in the band all four years in high school. I was taught to play the 2nd French horn. Being in the band was enjoyable. The whole school seemed to really like the band. I went from freshman to sophomore to junior to the senior band.

While in high school I met Delores Williams, who became my best friend. She was also one of The Gospelettes (singing trio). I had other close friends in school and at church.

In our church we were taught not to marry other denominations. When I was 17 years old, I met a young man named Luther Strong. Even though I was engaged to another young man, named Payton. I really found myself enjoying Luther more so.

I had been introduced to him right after he was out of the army by his cousin Florence who had become a good friend. After meeting Luther, I wrote Payton and told him I had met someone else that I really loved. He wrote me back and told me not to get serious about this guy because we had plans to get married.

However, after graduating from Vashon High School in 1955, I ended up marrying Luther Strong on February 19, 1956. We had a beautiful wedding at my church (507 South Jefferson). My pastor's wife helped me arrange my wedding (Sister Earline Ward). My wedding party consisted of, Leroy Logan (Luther's best man and cousin), Florence Carr (his cousin), George Watson (my cousin), Floyda Tate (my cousin), James Ward, Jr (Ring bearer), Ramona Watson (flower girl) and my little sister; Levenne. My Aunt Surveyor Proctor held the wedding reception at her home.

On my wedding night, I found out just what I had gotten myself into. My husband stayed out that night drinking with his cousin Leroy. I cried most of that night. I had to make a decision whether I was going to stick with my marriage or go back and be worried with my Aunt Jennie V. I decided to try to stay with my husband.

With many ups and downs, I stayed and prayed that the Lord would bless me with children. Soon God answered my prayers. My first daughter, Macie Marie, was born April 23, 1957. My second daughter Sherri Renee (called Sherri Rene) was born August 4, 1958. My third daughter Vanessa Bonita (called Bonnie) was born August 23, 1959. After Bonnie was born, I really realized that I needed to really get my spiritual life intact. I had already accepted Christ into my life but I had a hunger and thirst for more of the Lord. After Bonnie was a few months old, I began attending church frequently. I went to the altar and received a tremendous blessing. I also spoke in tongues. But I still wanted more of the Lord because as a child I really did not understand what it meant to be filled with the Holy Ghost.

One morning after giving my children breakfast and fixing my husband's lunch (he took his lunch to work), I made up my mind that I was going to seek the Lord as never before. I went into the Living Room and got on my knees and began praying. Some of the things I was asking God for: (1) to be filled completely with the Holy Ghost, (2) I wanted to experience having all nine gifts of the spirit because I wanted to be like people that I had witnessed using the ministry of the gifts of the Holy Spirit. I was praying earnestly and sincerely with all my heart, the year 1959. My encounter with the Holy Trinity, God the Father, Jesus the son and the precious Holy Ghost.

Suddenly, I felt the Holy Trinity enter the room. I began to feel a soothing warmth as my body began to shake. My hands felt like they were plugged into electrifying objects. I could no longer speak English; I began to sing in the holy language. I stood to my feet, but I began to dance around the living room. As I was singing this language, I could hear the heavenly host or angels singing along with me.

My two oldest daughters were playing in the water in the bathroom. I danced to the bathroom and lightly tapped them and they ran out right away.

I looked in the mirror and then I felt my hands being lifted. What a glorious day! I went to the phone to call my Aunt Mary. When she answered I was speaking in tongues. She called my name Georgia, I said yes. I am filled with the Holy Ghost. She said that's good and I think she said Keep praising the Lord.

That whole day I was anointed and felt so wonderful, I prayed "Lord I feel like I want to be with you, in heaven, if there is anything coming against me, to make me turn from you in my future, please take me now."

When my husband returned from work. I even felt different about him. I felt more understanding of his drinking habit. My whole life was changed. At night when I dreamed, I saw things that would happen the next day. I even knew who would be coming to my house.

A few days later, I felt led to go down to our neighborhood store and pray for the owner that had a stroke. So, I did, while I was praying for him, he began saying "your prayer is lost, I am not healed." He repeated that about twice. I did not know how to command that spirit to leave him and command his healing so I told his wife, if he would believe he would be healed. A neighbor (Mrs. Brown) came into the store, so I left and went home. A few minutes after, I came home there was a knock on my door. I went to the door and Mrs. Brown (my neighbor) was standing there. I invited her in and she started telling me, "Mrs. Strong, when I came into the store, I looked at you and there was a bright light shining around you. So, I came in so you could pray for me. I have been in the hospital to have surgery for locked bowels and I am still having trouble with that condition. I looked at her and I told her I would pray for her. Then I started singing.

Come in to my heart
Come in to my heart
Come in to my heart, Lord Jesus
Come in, come in today please come in oh Lord
I pray
Please, Come in to my heart Lord Jesus

Then I laid my right hand on her forehead and prayed that she would be healed. While I was praying for her, she suddenly said, I have to go. She left out quickly. About 30 minutes, she called me and said, while you were praying for me, I felt something break loose in me. I had to leave right away. When I got home, I went right to the bathroom and had a normal bowel movement. I am healed. I said praise God.

That Friday night, I went to church and had an unusual experience. There was one man in the audience that would start shouting out loudly whenever our pastor was preaching. We were all praising God and dancing. I found myself dancing around him and speaking in tongues (almost rebuking). Soon the service was over.

Sunday night while in service, I was sitting in my seat and I started shaking just as I had when I first received the baptism of the Holy Ghost. I felt as if someone was lifting me out of my seat. I started walking toward one of our members, which had leprosy. When I got to her the spirit spoke and said go into her and command her to be healed. But then another spirit said, everyone is looking at you. If you do that and she is not healed it will be shameful. I then walked over to her and laid hands on her. Instead of following what God had given me to do, I began speaking in tongues (which had been given me - gift of tongues) then I went back to my seat.

When I returned to my seat, I started shaking and I saw myself lifted over the audience and I looked down and saw a grave and I heard a voice saying Ward. I began shaking my head in a no position because I thought that our pastor Elder James Ward was going to die.

The next week, our pastor's father, Ward Senior died. So, I understood my vision. Things took definite turn since I was disobedient to the Lord. Satan attacked my mind every day. I would get out of the bed and go to the mirror to see if I had leprosy. Then I started telling people that I talked to their faults.

Everyone became upset with me. But I could not help myself. Two of my aunts came over and took me to a spiritualist doctor. When he called me in the room, I went in and started knocking things over. He called my aunts and told them to get me out of there. I remember feeling that he was of the devil.

So, one of my aunts took me to the number one city hospital. I was talking to the doctor and telling him about spiritual occurrences. He immediately signed me in the hospital.

While in the hospital a lady kept coming to me asking me to pray with her. One day she came and I prayed for her. She fell out and started rolling over. Then numerous patients started coming in the room. As they came in, I felt that it was many different spirits entering the room.

Soon the lady jumped up from the floor and started running down the corridors hollering and tearing her clothes. The nurses started running after her and caught her. One nurse told me they were going to give her a shot. I replied that is not going to help her because this is a spiritual battle. But to my surprise they were able to help her. Then she was calm but she began tormenting me, telling me that one of us was going out of there dead.

Every time the doctor talked to me; I would tell him about spiritual things I was experiencing naturally he did not understand. So, he ordered shock treatment for me. Those treatments felt like I was dying when they applied them and when they were finished, I felt lost and did not even know who I was. Finally, they decided they would discontinue the shock treatments.

While I was hospitalized, my Aunt Mary would keep my three daughters. She was very protective of them. She even trained my two youngest daughters to use the potty chair.

I was in and out of the hospital between 1959 and 1960. On July 4, 1960, I received a gate pass and my husband came and picked me up. During my stay I conceived my son, DeAndre Luther Strong, born March 19, 1961. I was in the hospital and when he was born, I was unable to come home so my Aunt Mary came out to get him and took him to her house with my three daughters.

I was in the hospital so much until Aunt Mary could not continue keeping my children. My husband Luther then took them to his mother (Susie Strong) and his sister Carrie Strong). They kept them safe. Then when they could not keep them anymore his cousin Florence took care of them. Other people helped to take care of them as well.

The doctors had prescribed a medicine for me that made me feel like a zombie. One medicine broke me out in a small rash. So, I would not take the medicine because I wanted to be divinely healed. They tried different medicines; some helped and some hindered. One time when I was experiencing an anxiety attack, my Aunt Surveyor Proctor took me to hospital number one. When we went in to talk to the doctor, the doctor asked me if I was taking my medicine. I said no, because my aunt told me not to take the medicine but to be healed.

While she was trying to explain herself to the doctor, I left out of the room and went out and caught a cab home. When my husband came to the door, he was shocked and asked where Aunt Vee was.

I told him she was at the hospital. She later told my husband that they wanted to keep her.

Trip to California

After being out of the hospital a few years, one of my stepsisters living in California sent me tickets to move to California. So, I decided to move to California. I packed all my children's clothing and my clothes and we prepared to take the train there. When we arrived in California, some of the family picked us up from the train station.

For about a week, things went all right and then the over anxiety struck me and I started telling them all the things that they were doing wrong. They started hitting me and my mother said let's take her to Reverend Allen's. So, they piled me in the car while hitting and beating me then one of my sisters twisted my wrist, even though that was over 40 years ago I still have pains occasionally in that wrist (my right wrist). I was trying to defend myself by fighting back.

When we arrived at Reverend Allen's, my clothes were all torn and they then put me on a stretcher so they could push me up to Rev. Allen. When it was my turn to be prayed for, he came over and started putting his hands on my head. I remember saying to him, the Holy Ghost is here so you don't have to pray. He then caught my hair and gave it a yank. Then he told them to take me away.

When we left from there my sisters was dragging me pulling me to the car, they took me to the Los

Angeles Hospital. When I went in to talk to the doctor, he looked at me and wanted to know what had happened to me. I told him I had been beaten. They signed me in and a few days later they transferred me to Camarillo Hospital. While I was in Camarillo, I started singing with their jazz band.

One day the doctor told me, that they had decided to fly me back to St. Louis and I would have to leave my children at my mother's house. I told him I did not want to leave my children there because they were being mistreated. My mother had told me she was going to make my children like slaves to her children.

It was a nurse in the room with the doctor and she said do you know anyone else out in California besides your family. Then I thought of my best friend, Georgianne Kincade and her family. They had moved from St. Louis to California. The nurse took down her name and started searching for her phone number. She told me that when and if she contacted her, she would come and tell me. A few weeks went on. Finally, one day the nurse came and told me she had talked to Georgianne. I talked to Georgianne by phone and told her what was happening so she said she would be out there. The doctor then asked me what was my relationship with Georgianne. I told him we had a very good relationship. I had kept her children and one of her daughters was my God child. A few days later, Georgianne and Mary Ann, my God child, arrived at the hospital. The doctor sent the nurse to get me. When I came in the room, Mary Ann ran to me and gave me a big hug. Then the doctor told me he knew then that we were good friends.

The doctor then explained to Georgianne what the problem was. Georgianne told him that she and her family loved me and would do everything possible to help me and my children.

I was supposed to sing with the jazz band on t.v. that next day or night (Somewhere Over the Rainbow), but I cancelled it because Georgianne and Mary Ann wanted me to go home with them. So, I got my things and went with them.

Georgianne told me, that the day before the nurse called her, she had started to get a private phone. If she had, there would have been no way I could get in touch with her. After arriving at Georgianne's home she told her husband to take me over to my mother's house to get my children and their things.

When we got there and knocked on the door one of my sisters came to the door. I saw two of my children standing behind her. My stepfather also came to the door. Mr. Kincade then told him that we had come to get my children. My mother first objected but then started sending them out. One of my sisters then started throwing their clothes out on their lawn. Soon we were settled in the car. Georgianne and her children were glad to see us.

The doctor had told Georgianne that if things went all right, she would not have to bring me back to the hospital. So, I called my husband in St. Louis and told him we wanted to come back to St. Louis. He soon sent tickets and we prepared to leave California.

Back in St. Louis

Things went back to normal except then my two oldest daughters had started attending school; first grade and kindergarten. I still at times had problems of anxiety but I had begun taking my medicine.

I began to teach my children songs to sing in church. We started back going to Kossuth Temple Church of God in Christ. The Lord was really blessing my children's voices. So soon we were called the Strong Family Singers. We started holding standard programs at one of the neighborhood churches (Rev. Mullins). The money we received helped us to pay for a piano. We were soon singing at various churches. One night we were asked by brother Leonard Morris to sing at the Coliseum. Other singers were there that had records out. The Lord blessed our voices. After the service, the group who had recordings asked if we had recordings. We had many opportunities to sing at various places. My Aunt Surveyor Proctor took us out of town to appear on programs with them. We also won second place singing at Forest Park Community College Talent Show.

On one occasion, the bishop's son Wadell Campbell really fell in love with us. He called me mom and my daughters his sisters and my son his brother. He soon came to St. Louis from Chicago to spend some time with us. He came on three occasions.

I still was having problems but they were not as severe. The Lord had blessed me to contact an agency called J.V.S. (Jewish Vocational Service) and they went all out to help me. They paid for a training program. They also paid for me to have surgery on my left ear. I had a very severe fever when I was young that had affected my hearing. After the surgery I could hear really well in my left ear. Then they started giving me an allowance to go through a training program clerical which included Dictaphone typing and filing and switchboard training. Mrs. Dorothy Checkett a very exceptional teacher who taught me to speed type. I finished her class typing 60 words per minute.

I had spent so much time in the hospital. But whenever, I was out, I would start my children back to singing and the Lord blessed me and gave me a real good counselor (Mr. Leon Cecil). He made me this promise, "I am going to get you a job if I have to drive you all over St. Louis in a truck." Mr. Cecil was really dedicated to his work of helping people.

Soon the Lord blessed me and my children to move in a house. After being in the house, Mr. Cecil took me to Concordia Publishing House on Jefferson. He took me to the customer service department where I talked to Mr. Benz. He told me he had an opening for a Dictaphone specialist and asked if I could handle that position. I told him I could so he hired me after a typing test.

I really enjoyed working there as my children were in school all day. I was really impressed with one employee there. He was always talking on the phone telling people what should be written in bible books. He told me the way to remember the 1st 5 books in the bible- GELND (Genesis, Exodus, Leviticus, Numbers and Deuteronomy). He also could speak different languages. I soon felt lead to change churches. So, I started attending Kennerly Temple Church of God in Christ where a young anointed Evangelist was holding revival. Her name was Maria Gardner. God was really working through this young woman. After the revival closed, I talked to the pastor (also named Ward) about becoming a member there. He immediately took my family and me.

A few months afterward we joined I had to go to Homer Phillips Hospital for DNC surgery. At that time, I was unable to work when I came home from the hospital, I had a serious talk with my husband about his behavior and his throwing away his money by drinking and gambling. I told him he had to stop or he would have to leave. He decided he would leave because he was expecting a big check that weekend. When he left, I told my children that he wasn't coming back. I felt somewhat worried about the consequences. But I also felt relieved. When he left, we did not have any food or money and I had just come from the hospital a few days beforehand.

While attending Kennerly Temple, I had acquired many friends because we sang as a family group and I also sang in the choir with my four children. One real friend was the pastor's wife and another young lady, Rose Marie Mallett was a real true friend. I called her and told her my predicament. She and her husband Roosevelt came over and brought some food. She advised me to tell Pastor Ward what I was experiencing. I called the pastor's wife and told her my problem. She was very encouraging and said she would tell the pastor. One of my aunts called and I told her what was happening. She told Helen Lumpkins, a pastor's wife, and a gospel singer. Then Rose Marie Mallett came over and took me to the social security office. I was able to apply for $128.00 food stamps right away. Rose Marie paid the co-payment and I received the stamps right away.

After returning home with groceries, I received more phone calls. God was pouring blessings on my children and me. I had so much joy in my soul from all of the blessings. A community agency contacted me and they brought a gift of $100.00. Three of the members of the church came to the house bringing food already cooked—fried chicken, mixed greens and baked sweet potatoes and corn bread. Whenever I would leave the house on errands, people would catch up with me and slip money in my hand various times.

That same week my husband called asking if I needed food. I told him God blessed me with food plus $128.00 in food stamps. He said, "Give me some food." God proved to me that my decision about my husband was right.

God continued to bless me when my husband left. The house was going into foreclosure and my phone was scheduled for disconnection. Our lights and gas bill were behind. But Pastor Ward called me up that Sunday and told the members what I was going through. They started rushing to the table. Pastor Ward had told me if I didn't receive enough in the offering then he would write a check to cover the remaining part to pay on the house to prevent the foreclosure.

I was so touched by all of the blessings God was pouring in. Yes, I truly thank God for how he blessed my four children and me. The Lord blessed me to get another job as an executive secretary at the Human Development Corporation. The house we lived in needed numerous repairs. So I decided to move to an apartment, on the south (Arco). A few weeks after we moved, one of the members asked me if I needed a car. I told her yes. But I would need to take some driving lessons. She came over to my home and picked me up to take me to her husband's job. He was a car salesman. When I arrived, the owner took me to look at a yellow mustang. I really liked it so I filled out the application to purchase the car.

When we went back to get the car, she asked me if I wanted to drive so even though I was a little leery I had taken driving lessons in high school. I got behind the wheel, but before we had gone a block, she decided that she would take over the driving. God was also blessing us spiritually. One day after school me and my children was praying in our living room and God began pouring out his spirit upon all of us. My four children received the Holy Spirit and began to speak in tongues. Soon after that occurrence they were baptized at Kennerly Temple C.O.G.I.C

.

Before I really was driving the car, I let my neighbor who lived on the first floor drive it. She was happy to drive the car to take her children to school and also my children. One day I came home and her little son was sitting on the front stairs. He called me and said, "Mommy took our car and she would be back." I knew then it was time for me to start driving. So, I asked Rev. Stokes, a fellow employee who worked with me if he would give me driving lessons; he agreed. He was willing to do it in return for me helping him with some paperwork.

So, I began my lessons late in the evening. We lived near Forest Park so we would drive there to practice. Soon I was able to get my permit. Then I started driving at night down Chouteau Blvd. Soon I applied for my driving license and passed the test. After I was confident, I started teaching my children to drive. They learned quickly. Then they took the test to get their license. They finally passed the test.

While living on the south side my children had to catch two busses to get to school, which meant they had to get up before daybreak. One day while they were coming home from Roosevelt High School, an older boy started a fight with my youngest daughter Vanessa. When they were getting ready to board the second bus, he caught up with them and started punching them. They ran into a restaurant and the proprietor called the police. By that time, I had made it to my house. I received a call from the hospital. I rushed and left home to get to the hospital. When I arrived there, my daughter Sherri had been punched in the mouth and was bleeding. My youngest daughter Vanessa had a swollen face. But God has spared their lives.

After that incident, I really began praying and asking God to bless us to move to a place where they could walk to school that was near our home.

One day I felt the urge to go for a bus ride to the end of the line. I caught the Forest Park Bus. I was relaxing and I always keep a prayer on my mind. Finally, the bus turned on Eager Road in Brentwood. The driver said he was taking a break. I got off the bus and started walking around. I really liked what I saw. There were so many nice houses and apartments. I saw people of different races there. I decided to ask someone for directions to the leasing office. I went in and a lady named Mrs. Church came to wait on me. She gave me a form to fill out but she said most residents were either students or worked full time. I told her I was a student and I was also employed. I was attending Forest Park Community College and I worked for the Human Development Corporation.

Mrs. Church then said I would need a co-signer with a good credit rating. So, I left the application with her and left the office. I was really praying that my children and me would get to live there. When I arrived home the Lord began giving me directions on what to do. Just as he led me, I called Rev. Wesley, the pastor of the small church my children and I was working with. I told him about the place I had found in Brentwood, MO and told him that I wanted to move there. I also told him that I needed a co-signer in order to qualify for the apartment. He asked me when did I need him to go out there. I told him as soon as possible.

When we arrived there Mrs. Church was there to wait on us. She began talking to Pastor Wesley and they seemed to really be agreeing. He told her that when he came to St. Louis all the land where their apartments were was cow pasture. She smiled and then we proceeded with the lease. I needed to pay two months lease note. I knew at that time I did not have the money but I told Mrs. Church that I would be back with the money. I thanked Pastor Wesley and he took me to my house. After I got home the

Lord directed me to make phone calls. I had good credit with some of my neighbors from North St. Louis. I called Mrs. Walker and told her how much I needed and she said okay. Then I called Mrs. Thomas, she also said alright.

I went to get the money and then I was ready to go and finalize the lease. My children and I went to Brentwood because I wanted to show them where we were moving. They were so impressed with Audubon Park and especially so when they found out their school were just a few blocks from our house. Finally, the day came to move in. I had asked two other friends to contact movers that they knew. So off to Brentwood my children and me moved. My oldest daughter had married a young man named Edward. But when we moved, she came out to see the place. She really loved it. It was like living in paradise. The children would have the chance to attend seemingly private school. All three of my children would attend the same school. My son was the youngest and had not graduated from Elementary school. But he also was enrolled at Brentwood high school. The Lord really opened up the windows of heaven to us. It was so restful living there. Some people did not lock their doors. It was so beautiful living there. They had tennis courts, swimming pools, play areas all over the complex. Laundromats it was like a separate city. I always felt so relaxed when the bus would turn going into Audubon Park.

My children liked their school. It was a totally different way of life. Instead of the children dressing up to go to school, they wore tennis shoes, jeans, and t-shirts. That was a tremendous blessing because they now could concentrate more on their studies instead of the clothes they wore. They also excelled in their schoolwork. My second daughter, Sherri brought her grades up to honor roll status. My youngest daughter, Bonnie joined the drill team and soon became the captain of the drill team. My son excelled in sports, a basketball star, football star. He played the bass guitar for the choir. He also excelled in Karate. Their father had the chance to attend some of their activities, one night at the football game he was sitting next to the mayor watching their sons play ball. They all had summer jobs. Yes, God's hand was truly upon our lives. I soon found out that the government programs that I worked for was phasing out. So, I knew I would be out of a job. Although vocational rehab was helping me, I needed another job. One day after prayer the Lord led me to go to our administrative office. So, I went and talked to the manager's assistant. I told her that I might have to move due to a decrease in funds. She then said why don't you work here for us. We need a head-leasing agent and we are opening one of the apartments for a display. That's where the leasing office will be. So, I filled out an application for work and the next week I began my job as the head-leasing agent of Audobon Park Apartments. I found out that they had over 107 or more acres and they had 1400 apartments. She also told me that my rent would be decreased quite a lot. They had golf carts to drive to show the apartments to potential tenants. But soon they purchased a brand-new car to show tenants the apartments. They had at least 700 one-bedroom apartments and other 700 was a mixture of two bedrooms and 3-bedroom apartments. Yes, it was like living in paradise and it was so beautiful and peaceful. After being employed there for two years I changed apartments. They were always striving to make improvements in the living arrangements.

My third apartment was a lovely wall-to-wall carpeting town home, 1st and 2nd floors. After living there, a while my boss (Mr. Streiler) called me into the office. He told me that an agency had been there to talk to them about sponsoring someone in an apartment. They would pay over half of the lease note. The only problem, I would have to give up the super deluxe apartment at 9185 Wrenwood for a regular 3 bedroom with or without carpeting. So, I agreed and we moved a block up to Swallow. All of the streets had bird names. As time went on, we were really enjoying our stay in Brentwood.

My second daughter, Sherri graduated. The mayor presented her an outstanding certificate for an outstanding honor roll student. She graduated in 1976 from high school and enrolled in Harris Stowe College. She met a young man there from Ethiopia. They are now married and have two wonderful children; a daughter, Lea Rahael Girma and son, Christian Azana Bekele-Girma. They are both brilliant children and blessed by God. Sherri's son Christian is a miracle child.

The doctors wanted to perform a hysterectomy before he was conceived. But God did not permit it. Sherri threatened to lose her son during the pregnancy. At birth, he only weighed 4 lbs. and 6 ounces. My daughter and son-in-law asked if I would babysit. I agreed promptly because Christian was such a special child. For his infant years, I enjoyed keeping him. When Christian started Headstart at Praise Tabernacle, I would pick him up from school. God truly blessed Christian and he excelled in his studies. God is still blessing him. Today, he is 6ft tall and an honor student in high school.

I also enjoyed Sherri's daughter Lea as a baby. I did not babysit with her because I was working full time at Washington University working as a secretary for three doctors (Dental Science, Conjoint Science and Behavioral Science). I spent a lot of time with Lea in her infancy years and when she started school, I would pick her up afterwards. When Lea was a young teenager, I enjoyed her helping me to sponsor a program at Northview Nursing Home. We would pass out Christian tracts to the residents. Lea also played and sang a song for the residents (God is so good). There were two other missionaries that assisted me.

I also graduated in 1979 from Forest Park Community College. I received an Associate of

Liberal Arts Degree. My youngest daughter, Bonnie, was married but decided she wanted to go to Excelsior Springs to attend school. She was blessed to go through the Job Corp where she really excelled, graduated with much training- CPA, Nursing and Nursing Assistant. She received a dietician training also. God really had his hands on my family.

My oldest daughter decided after marrying to go back to school. She finished going to school day and evenings. She also graduated in 1976 as an honor student. Then she went to a secretarial school where she completed and was called by many jobs for employment.

God had promised me that we would be blessed to stay in Brentwood until my children graduated from high school. When we first moved there, most people thought we would only be there a few months. God really worked miracles in our lives. My son also graduated from Brentwood high school. He was a star basketball player. They had write-ups about him in the newspapers calling him "Dunking Dee." We lived in Brentwood from 1974 to 1981. Yes, I know how God's hand was and still is upon our lives.

There are so many other things that transpired in our lives that time will not permit me to tell. But I know that there is this natural world and there is a spiritual world. For during my stay in hospitals, patients that had different spirits promoting them encountered me. On one occasion a young man came up to me cursing and I said, "The blood of Jesus is against you Satan." He became furious. So, it was almost time to go to lunch. So, I went into the lunchroom with others.

When I came back in, the young man that had cursed me was lying on a stretcher fastened down with straps. I asked someone what happened to him. They said he was in a fight. The baddest man on that ward had beaten him up. Finally, they let him go. He then came straight to me and said, "I am sorry for the things I said to you. Pray that the blood of Jesus is not against me. I forgave him." Then there was a very stout and tall girl. She was sitting at a table playing cards and she continued to curse. I don't know what I said but I spoke in tongues. She looked at me and jumped up to attack me. But again, the baddest man in the bunch grabbed her and kept her from attacking me. The reason I called him "the baddest man on the ward," he was brought to the hospital in handcuffs by policemen. After a few days, I was able to talk to him. He told me the reason he was brought in by policemen; he had planned to kill a man that had murdered his sister.

I then told him about Mrs. Gore, 1st lady of Christ Southern Mission Baptist Church. She was a volunteer at the hospital. Mrs. Gore would come in and give gifts to the patients.

I told him one of her daughters was shot and injured badly. I asked him if he would like to talk to her. He said yes. When she came on our ward, I told her about the young man who wanted to talk to her. She agreed to talk to him. I walked with her to meet him. They were introduced and set down to talk. I did not stay to hear the conversation. A few days later, I talked to him. This man shared that he wrote a letter to his pastor asking him to come to the hospital and pray with him. He also shared with me, he decided to return to church, praise God. It seemed that the baddest man on the ward had accepted Christ in his life.

Yes, even though I had been disobedient, God was still with me protecting me. Yes, also protecting my children. God was blessing us in every way in Brentwood.

One day we were walking around at West Roads. There were two children selling raffle tickets. They approached me and said these tickets are only one dollar. So, I said, I will buy one. Then I smiled and said make sure I win the half cow. A few weeks passed by and we were getting low on food. Then I received a phone call. The lady on the phone told me that she was calling me in reference to a ticket purchased a few weeks earlier. I said yes, then she said you are our winner of the half cow. She told me the name of the grocery store. where I could pick it up and gave me the phone number and grocers name.

So, I called him and he asked me how I wanted the half cow cut, so I told him I would call him back. I then called Pastor Wesley, which was also a butcher and told him the good news and asked him if he would call and tell them how to cut the half cow. He said yes. I then called the owner of the store and he told me he would get it ready for me to pick up. He later called me and said it was ready. So, I had been blessed with another car after taking the mustang back because it needed repairs every month.

I drove down to the store. I have never seen so many packages of beef. We had every kind of steak, ribs, and ground beef. There was just about every kind of cut that can be made from a whole half cow.

The Lord blessed me to be a blessing to relatives and friends with that Tremendous Blessing. Yes, God's hand has been upon my life and the lives of my children. My son was in a very serious accident on his job where he worked as an operator of a forklift truck. He has had two very serious surgeries and he is still having physical, muscular and nerve pains. Through it all, God spared his life. My son is blessed to have five children from two previous marriages before his injury, four daughters and one son. His children look up to him for spiritual guidance. I am so thankful and grateful to God for my entire family and for his numerous blessings. Yes, God's hand is upon my life and the lives of my family. This book just tells of some of God's blessings.

In closing, I would like to encourage all of the readers of this book to give their lives to Christ and put their trust in God. For God is real.

Ephesians 3:20,21

20 - Now unto him that is able to do exceedingly abundantly above all that we ask or think according to the power that worketh in us.

21 - Unto him be the glory in the church by Christ Jesus throughout all ages. World without End.

Amen